Potato Head

by Grace Hansen

Abdo Kids Jumbo is an Imprint of Abdo Kids
abdobooks.com

abdobooks.com

Published by Abdo Kids, a division of ABDO, P.O. Box 398166, Minneapolis, Minnesota 55439.
Copyright © 2023 by Abdo Consulting Group, Inc. International copyrights reserved in all countries.
No part of this book may be reproduced in any form without written permission from the publisher.
Abdo Kids Jumbo™ is a trademark and logo of Abdo Kids.

Printed in China.

102022

012023

Photo Credits: Alamy, Everette Collection, Getty Images, Shutterstock PREMIER

Production Contributors: Teddy Borth, Jennie Forsberg, Grace Hansen
Design Contributors: Candice Keimig, Pakou Moua

Library of Congress Control Number: 2022937182
Publisher's Cataloging-in-Publication Data

Names: Hansen, Grace, author.

Title: Potato head / by Grace Hansen

Description: Minneapolis, Minnesota : Abdo Kids, 2023 | Series: Toy mania! | Includes online resources and
    index.

Identifiers: ISBN 9781098264314 (lib. bdg.) | ISBN 9781098264871 (ebook) | ISBN 9781098265151
    (Read-to-Me ebook)

Subjects: LCSH: Mr. Potato Head (Trademark)--Juvenile literature. | Potatoes--Juvenile literature. | Toys--
    Juvenile literature. | Hasbro, Inc.--Juvenile literature.

Classification: DDC 688.72--dc23

Table of Contents

Potato Head

Everyone loves the tough spud from the *Toy Story* movies. But Mr. Potato Head entertained kids long before his big screen debut!

Food Fun!

In 1949, George Lerner sat at the dinner table with his family. His two boys, Franklin and David, played with their food more than they ate it. This gave George an idea!

Potatoes
again?

George created the Funny

Faces for Food kit. It included

three-dimensional plastic

pieces. The parts could stick

into fruits and vegetables.

George tried to sell his idea
to toy companies. But many
thought it was wasteful. People
were used to **rationing** foods
during World War II. The thought
of kids poking and prodding
fresh foods seemed silly.

HOW TO SHOP WITH WAR RATION BOOK TWO
... to Buy Canned, Bottled and Frozen Fruits and Vegetables;
Dried Fruits, Juices and all Canned Soups
CEILING PRICES
YOUR POINT ALLOWANCE MUST LAST FOR THE FULL
Plan How Many Points You Will Use Each Time Before
BUY EARLY IN THE WEEK
First Month's Points
A 8 B 8 C 8
A 5 B 5 C 5
B 2 C 2
B
11

Finally, in 1952, Hasbro bought George's idea. Hasbro decided potatoes were the perfect veggie. So, they gave the toy a new name. Mr. Potato Head starred in the first toy television ad the same year.

Mr. POTATO HEAD
FUNNY-FACE KIT
PEPPER
BEET
ORANGE
APPLE
ANY F
MAKES
57a MR. POTATO HEAD
mint condition set of the original
toy manufactured by Hasbro Toy Com-
pany in 1950...this was the first
toy ever advertised on TV
EAD
AMILY

In 1953, Mrs. Potato Head joined in on the fun. The next year, Brother Spud and Sister Yam were born. The Potato Heads were a hit!

BABY POTATO HEAD
The HASBRO Guide to
America's TOP TEN TOYS!
Mr. and Mrs. POTATO HEAD
the joyful toy of 1001 faces!
Hasbro Toys are truly inspirational—and there are none finer!
15

Fantastic Plastic

In the 1960s and 1970s, the US government had new rules. Selling sharp toys to kids became illegal. So, in 1964, Hasbro created a plastic head and body with pre-made holes.

Mr. POTATO
ANY FRUI
MAK

The Potato Head we know today took shape in 1974. Hasbro combined the body and head pieces into one. The company also doubled the size of its plastic pieces. Now kids of all ages could play with Mr. Potato Head!

In 1995, George Lerner died. But his ideas lived on. The same year, Mr. Potato Head shined in *Toy Story*. The Potato Heads continue to **amuse** kids both in person and on screen.

Mr. Potato Head
60
Mr. Potato Head
new
P
MR. POTATO HEAD
PLAYSKOOL

More Facts

- After the television **ad**, more than 1 million Mr. Potato Head kits sold in the first year.

- Mr. Potato Head has had many fun costumes over the years. Hasbro has released Darth Tater, R2-POTATOO, Spider Spud, and many more!

- Mr. Potato Head was **inducted** into the National Toy Hall of Fame in 2000.

Glossary

ad – short for advertisement, a public notice that tells people about products, services, or things that are happening.

amuse – to hold the interest of in a pleasant way.

debut – a first appearance in a film.

inducted – brought in as a member.

rationing – limiting the use of.

spud – a potato.

three-dimensional – having depth, height, and width.

Index

Visit **abdokids.com** to access crafts, games, videos, and more!